BEST PLACES
TRAVEL JOURNAL

SASQUATCH BOOKS
SEATTLE

Printed in the United States of America
Published by Sasquatch Books
Distributed by PGW/Perseus
15 14 13 12 11 10 09 08 07   9 8 7 6 5 4 3 2 1

Cover design: Kate Basart/Union Pageworks
Interior design & composition: Kate Basart/Union Pageworks
Map: © Map Resources

ISBN-13: 978-1-57061-535-1
ISBN-10: 1-57061-535-7

Sasquatch Books
119 South Main Street, Suite 400
Seattle, WA 98104
(206) 467-4300
www.sasquatchbooks.com
custserv@sasquatchbooks.com

CONTENTS

YOU'RE THE BEST CRITIC

As the publisher of the well-loved BEST PLACES® travel guide series, we've always depended on the contributions of locals to determine which establishments to include in our guides. Through our readers we discover hidden treasures, special experiences, and what really goes on inside a restaurant when an established critic isn't there.

Over the years thousands of readers have responded to our reviews. We've heard about hotels and B&Bs that readers feel have been unfairly slighted, as well as critically acclaimed restaurants in which diners have consumed less-than-outstanding meals. Such feedback has been invaluable to us as we've compiled our guidebooks; now we want to give you a chance to record your own experiences.

We invite you to take this journal along as you enjoy restaurants around your neighborhood, as you stay in hotels around the country, as you explore the hot shopping spots of the moment. Truly, there is no better critic out there than you. Who else can account for your personal tastes, your likes, your dislikes, the things you look for whenever you visit any restaurant, hotel, or store?

For your ease, we have divided this journal into several sections.

In **Places to Check Out**, create a running list of establishments you've heard about from friends, family, or the local paper, but haven't yet visited.

In the **Best Places to Eat, Stay**, and **Shop** sections, review restaurants, lodgings, and stores using the preformatted pages and guided review tools. In **Best Places to Stay**, there is an extra page to note memorable moments from your trip. And should you run out of room in any of those sections, check out **More Best Places** for additional space.

We wish you the BEST in all your future travels and critical ventures!

HOW TO USE THIS JOURNAL

STAR RATINGS Restaurants and lodgings can be rated on a scale of one to four stars (with half stars in between), based on quality, service, ambience, cleanliness, value, and general experience.

★★★★   The very best

★★★   Distinguished; many outstanding features

★★   Excellent; some wonderful qualities

★   A good place

PRICE RANGE The ranges for restaurants are based on dinner for two, including dessert and tip, but not alcohol. Lodging prices are based on one night's accomodations for two adults.

$$$$ Very expensive (more than $100 for dinner; more than $200 per night for lodging)

$$$ Expensive (between $65 and $100 for dinner; between $120 and $200 per night for lodging)

$$ Moderate (between $35 and $65 for dinner; between $80 and $120 per night for lodging)

$ Inexpensive (less than $35 for dinner; less than $80 per night for lodging)

HELPFUL ICONS Use these quick-reference symbols as you rate the best places to eat and stay:

🏃   **FAMILY FUN**   Places that are fun, easy, and great for kids.

🐷   **GOOD VALUE**   While not necessarily cheap, these spots offer a good deal for the cost.

💘   **ROMANTIC**   These places offer candlelight, atmosphere, intimacy, or other romantic qualities.

✓   **YOUR CHOICE**   Places you especially love.

PLACES TO CHECK OUT

NAME

LOCATION

RECOMMENDED BY

WHY GO

★ ★

NAME

LOCATION

RECOMMENDED BY

WHY GO

★ ★

NAME

LOCATION

RECOMMENDED BY

WHY GO

NAME

LOCATION

RECOMMENDED BY

WHY GO

★ ★

NAME

LOCATION

RECOMMENDED BY

WHY GO

★ ★

NAME

LOCATION

RECOMMENDED BY

WHY GO

NAME

LOCATION

RECOMMENDED BY

WHY GO

★ ★

NAME

LOCATION

RECOMMENDED BY

WHY GO

★ ★

NAME

LOCATION

RECOMMENDED BY

WHY GO

NAME

LOCATION

RECOMMENDED BY

WHY GO

★ ★

NAME

LOCATION

RECOMMENDED BY

WHY GO

★ ★

NAME

LOCATION

RECOMMENDED BY

WHY GO

NAME
....

LOCATION
....

RECOMMENDED BY
....

WHY GO
....

★ ★

NAME
....

LOCATION
....

RECOMMENDED BY
....

WHY GO
....

★ ★

NAME
....

LOCATION
....

RECOMMENDED BY
....

WHY GO
....

NAME

LOCATION

RECOMMENDED BY

WHY GO

★ ★

NAME

LOCATION

RECOMMENDED BY

WHY GO

★ ★

NAME

LOCATION

RECOMMENDED BY

WHY GO

NAME

....

LOCATION

....

RECOMMENDED BY

....

WHY GO

★ ★

NAME

....

LOCATION

....

RECOMMENDED BY

....

WHY GO

★ ★

NAME

....

LOCATION

....

RECOMMENDED BY

....

WHY GO

NAME

LOCATION

RECOMMENDED BY

WHY GO

★ ★

NAME

LOCATION

RECOMMENDED BY

WHY GO

★ ★

NAME

LOCATION

RECOMMENDED BY

WHY GO

NAME

LOCATION

RECOMMENDED BY

WHY GO

★ ★

NAME

LOCATION

RECOMMENDED BY

WHY GO

★ ★

NAME

LOCATION

RECOMMENDED BY

WHY GO

NAME

LOCATION

RECOMMENDED BY

WHY GO

★ ★

NAME

LOCATION

RECOMMENDED BY

WHY GO

★ ★

NAME

LOCATION

RECOMMENDED BY

WHY GO

NAME

LOCATION

RECOMMENDED BY

WHY GO

★ ★

NAME

LOCATION

RECOMMENDED BY

WHY GO

★ ★

NAME

LOCATION

RECOMMENDED BY

WHY GO

NAME

LOCATION

RECOMMENDED BY

WHY GO

★ ★

NAME

LOCATION

RECOMMENDED BY

WHY GO

★ ★

NAME

LOCATION

RECOMMENDED BY

WHY GO

NAME

LOCATION

RECOMMENDED BY

WHY GO

* *

NAME

LOCATION

RECOMMENDED BY

WHY GO

* *

NAME

LOCATION

RECOMMENDED BY

WHY GO

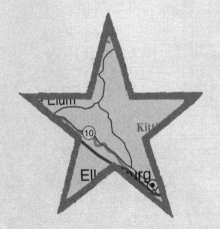

BEST PLACES TO EAT

☆ ☆ ☆ ☆

NAME .... RATING

TYPE OF CUISINE ....

LOCATION ....

ICONS: 🚻 🐷 💘 ✔   PRICE: $ $$ $$$ $$$$

THE FOOD
....

....

....

THE AMBIENCE
....

THE SERVICE
....

OTHER THOUGHTS
....

....

....

....

$ ($35 OR LESS FOR TWO) $$ ($35 TO $65 FOR TWO)
$$$ ($65 TO $100 FOR TWO) $$$$ (MORE THAN $100 FOR TWO)

16

☆ ☆ ☆ ☆

NAME .... RATING

TYPE OF CUISINE ....

LOCATION ....

ICONS: 👫 🐷 💘 ✔   PRICE: $ $$ $$$ $$$$

THE FOOD
....
....
....

THE AMBIENCE
....

THE SERVICE
....

OTHER THOUGHTS
....
....
....
....
....

$ ($35 OR LESS FOR TWO) $$ ($35 TO $65 FOR TWO)
$$$ ($65 TO $100 FOR TWO) $$$$ (MORE THAN $100 FOR TWO)

☆ ☆ ☆ ☆

NAME   RATING

TYPE OF CUISINE

LOCATION

ICONS: 🧍🧍 🐷 💘 ✓   PRICE: $ $$ $$$ $$$$

THE FOOD

THE AMBIENCE

THE SERVICE

OTHER THOUGHTS

$ ($35 OR LESS FOR TWO) $$ ($35 TO $65 FOR TWO)
$$$ ($65 TO $100 FOR TWO) $$$$ (MORE THAN $100 FOR TWO)

☆ ☆ ☆ ☆

NAME .... RATING

TYPE OF CUISINE ....

LOCATION ....

ICONS: 👫 🍲 💘 ✔   PRICE: $ $$ $$$ $$$$

THE FOOD
....
....
....

THE AMBIENCE
....

THE SERVICE
....

OTHER THOUGHTS
....
....
....
....

$ ($35 OR LESS FOR TWO) $$ ($35 TO $65 FOR TWO)
$$$ ($65 TO $100 FOR TWO) $$$$ (MORE THAN $100 FOR TWO)

☆ ☆ ☆ ☆

NAME   RATING

TYPE OF CUISINE

LOCATION

ICONS: 👫 🐷 💘 ✓   PRICE: $ $$ $$$ $$$$

THE FOOD

THE AMBIENCE

THE SERVICE

OTHER THOUGHTS

$ ($35 OR LESS FOR TWO) $$ ($35 TO $65 FOR TWO)
$$$ ($65 TO $100 FOR TWO) $$$$ (MORE THAN $100 FOR TWO)

☆ ☆ ☆ ☆

NAME .... RATING

TYPE OF CUISINE ....

LOCATION ....

ICONS: 👫 🐖 💘 ✔   PRICE: $ $$ $$$ $$$$

THE FOOD
....
....
....

THE AMBIENCE
....

THE SERVICE
....

OTHER THOUGHTS
....
....
....
....

$ ($35 OR LESS FOR TWO) $$ ($35 TO $65 FOR TWO)
$$$ ($65 TO $100 FOR TWO) $$$$ (MORE THAN $100 FOR TWO)

☆☆☆☆

NAME RATING

TYPE OF CUISINE

LOCATION

ICONS: 👫 🐖 💘 ✓ PRICE: $ $$ $$$ $$$$

THE FOOD

THE AMBIENCE

THE SERVICE

OTHER THOUGHTS

$ ($35 OR LESS FOR TWO) $$ ($35 TO $65 FOR TWO)
$$$ ($65 TO $100 FOR TWO) $$$$ (MORE THAN $100 FOR TWO)

☆ ☆ ☆ ☆

NAME .... RATING

TYPE OF CUISINE ....

LOCATION ....

ICONS: 🧒 🫖 💘 ✔   PRICE: $ $$ $$$ $$$$

THE FOOD
....
....
....
....

THE AMBIENCE
....

THE SERVICE
....

OTHER THOUGHTS
....
....
....
....

$ ($35 OR LESS FOR TWO) $$ ($35 TO $65 FOR TWO)
$$$ ($65 TO $100 FOR TWO) $$$$ (MORE THAN $100 FOR TWO)

☆ ☆ ☆ ☆

NAME   RATING

TYPE OF CUISINE

LOCATION

ICONS: 👫 🫖 💘 ✔   PRICE: $ $$ $$$ $$$$

THE FOOD

THE AMBIENCE

THE SERVICE

OTHER THOUGHTS

$ ($35 OR LESS FOR TWO) $$ ($35 TO $65 FOR TWO)
$$$ ($65 TO $100 FOR TWO) $$$$ (MORE THAN $100 FOR TWO)

☆ ☆ ☆ ☆

NAME   RATING

TYPE OF CUISINE

LOCATION

ICONS: 🚻 🐷 💘 ✓   PRICE: $ $$ $$$ $$$$

THE FOOD

THE AMBIENCE

THE SERVICE

OTHER THOUGHTS

$ ($35 OR LESS FOR TWO) $$ ($35 TO $65 FOR TWO)
$$$ ($65 TO $100 FOR TWO) $$$$ (MORE THAN $100 FOR TWO)

☆ ☆ ☆ ☆

NAME .... RATING

TYPE OF CUISINE ....

LOCATION ....
....

ICONS: 👫 🐷 💘 ✓   PRICE: $ $$ $$$ $$$$

THE FOOD
....
....
....
....

THE AMBIENCE
....
....

THE SERVICE
....
....

OTHER THOUGHTS
....
....
....
....
....

$ ($35 OR LESS FOR TWO) $$ ($35 TO $65 FOR TWO)
$$$ ($65 TO $100 FOR TWO) $$$$ (MORE THAN $100 FOR TWO)

☆ ☆ ☆ ☆

NAME .... RATING

TYPE OF CUISINE ....

LOCATION ....

ICONS: 🚹🚺 🐷 💘 ✓   PRICE: $ $$ $$$ $$$$

THE FOOD ....

....

....

THE AMBIENCE ....

....

THE SERVICE ....

....

OTHER THOUGHTS ....

....

....

....

....

$ ($35 OR LESS FOR TWO) $$ ($35 TO $65 FOR TWO)
$$$ ($65 TO $100 FOR TWO) $$$$ (MORE THAN $100 FOR TWO)

☆ ☆ ☆ ☆

NAME

RATING

TYPE OF CUISINE

LOCATION

ICONS: 🚻 🐷 🚀 ✓   PRICE: $ $$ $$$ $$$$

THE FOOD

THE AMBIENCE

THE SERVICE

OTHER THOUGHTS

$ ($35 OR LESS FOR TWO) $$ ($35 TO $65 FOR TWO)
$$$ ($65 TO $100 FOR TWO) $$$$ (MORE THAN $100 FOR TWO)

☆ ☆ ☆ ☆

NAME .... RATING

TYPE OF CUISINE ....

LOCATION ....

ICONS: 👫 🐷 💘 ✔   PRICE: $ $$ $$$ $$$$

THE FOOD
....
....
....

THE AMBIENCE
....

THE SERVICE
....

OTHER THOUGHTS
....
....
....
....

$ ($35 OR LESS FOR TWO) $$ ($35 TO $65 FOR TWO)
$$$ ($65 TO $100 FOR TWO) $$$$ (MORE THAN $100 FOR TWO)

☆ ☆ ☆ ☆

NAME   RATING

TYPE OF CUISINE

LOCATION

ICONS: 🏃 🐷 💘 ✓   PRICE: $ $$ $$$ $$$$

THE FOOD

THE AMBIENCE

THE SERVICE

OTHER THOUGHTS

$ ($35 OR LESS FOR TWO) $$ ($35 TO $65 FOR TWO)
$$$ ($65 TO $100 FOR TWO) $$$$ (MORE THAN $100 FOR TWO)

☆ ☆ ☆ ☆

NAME   RATING

TYPE OF CUISINE

LOCATION

ICONS: 🚻 🐷 💘 ✓   PRICE: $ $$ $$$ $$$$

THE FOOD

THE AMBIENCE

THE SERVICE

OTHER THOUGHTS

$ ($35 OR LESS FOR TWO) $$ ($35 TO $65 FOR TWO)
$$$ ($65 TO $100 FOR TWO) $$$$ (MORE THAN $100 FOR TWO)

☆ ☆ ☆ ☆

NAME .... RATING

TYPE OF CUISINE ....

LOCATION ....

ICONS: 🚸 🐷 🛸 ✓   PRICE: $ $$ $$$ $$$$

THE FOOD
....
....
....

THE AMBIENCE
....

THE SERVICE
....

OTHER THOUGHTS
....
....
....
....

$ ($35 OR LESS FOR TWO) $$ ($35 TO $65 FOR TWO)
$$$ ($65 TO $100 FOR TWO) $$$$ (MORE THAN $100 FOR TWO)

☆ ☆ ☆ ☆

NAME _____ RATING

TYPE OF CUISINE _____

LOCATION _____

ICONS: 👫 🐷 💘 ✓   PRICE: $ $$ $$$ $$$$

THE FOOD
_____
_____
_____

THE AMBIENCE
_____

THE SERVICE
_____

OTHER THOUGHTS
_____
_____
_____
_____

$ ($35 OR LESS FOR TWO) $$ ($35 TO $65 FOR TWO)
$$$ ($65 TO $100 FOR TWO) $$$$ (MORE THAN $100 FOR TWO)

☆ ☆ ☆ ☆

NAME .... RATING

TYPE OF CUISINE ....

LOCATION ....
....

ICONS: 👫 🐷 🚀 ✔   PRICE: $ $$ $$$ $$$$

THE FOOD
....
....
....

THE AMBIENCE
....

THE SERVICE
....

OTHER THOUGHTS
....
....
....
....
....

$ ($35 OR LESS FOR TWO) $$ ($35 TO $65 FOR TWO)
$$$ ($65 TO $100 FOR TWO) $$$$ (MORE THAN $100 FOR TWO)

☆ ☆ ☆ ☆

NAME   RATING

TYPE OF CUISINE

LOCATION

ICONS: 🚻 🐖 💘 ✓   PRICE: $ $$ $$$ $$$$

THE FOOD

THE AMBIENCE

THE SERVICE

OTHER THOUGHTS

$ ($35 OR LESS FOR TWO) $$ ($35 TO $65 FOR TWO)
$$$ ($65 TO $100 FOR TWO) $$$$ (MORE THAN $100 FOR TWO)

☆ ☆ ☆ ☆

NAME   RATING
....

TYPE OF CUISINE
....

LOCATION
....

ICONS: 👫 🐖 🚀 ✔   PRICE: $ $$ $$$ $$$$

THE FOOD
....
....
....

THE AMBIENCE
....
....

THE SERVICE
....
....

OTHER THOUGHTS
....
....
....
....
....

$ ($35 OR LESS FOR TWO) $$ ($35 TO $65 FOR TWO)
$$$ ($65 TO $100 FOR TWO) $$$$ (MORE THAN $100 FOR TWO)

☆ ☆ ☆ ☆

NAME   RATING

TYPE OF CUISINE

LOCATION

ICONS: 👫 🐷 💘 ✓   PRICE: $ $$ $$$ $$$$

THE FOOD

THE AMBIENCE

THE SERVICE

OTHER THOUGHTS

$ ($35 OR LESS FOR TWO) $$ ($35 TO $65 FOR TWO)
$$$ ($65 TO $100 FOR TWO) $$$$ (MORE THAN $100 FOR TWO)

☆ ☆ ☆ ☆

NAME   RATING

TYPE OF CUISINE

LOCATION

ICONS: 🧑‍🤝‍🧑 🐷 💘 ✓   PRICE: $ $$ $$$ $$$$

THE FOOD

THE AMBIENCE

THE SERVICE

OTHER THOUGHTS

$ ($35 OR LESS FOR TWO) $$ ($35 TO $65 FOR TWO)
$$$ ($65 TO $100 FOR TWO) $$$$ (MORE THAN $100 FOR TWO)

☆ ☆ ☆ ☆

NAME .... RATING

TYPE OF CUISINE ....

LOCATION ....

ICONS: 🏃🏃 🐷 💘 ✓   PRICE: $ $$ $$$ $$$$

THE FOOD
....

....

....

....

THE AMBIENCE
....

....

THE SERVICE
....

....

OTHER THOUGHTS
....

....

....

....

....

$ ($35 OR LESS FOR TWO) $$ ($35 TO $65 FOR TWO)
$$$ ($65 TO $100 FOR TWO) $$$$ (MORE THAN $100 FOR TWO)

☆ ☆ ☆ ☆

NAME   RATING

TYPE OF CUISINE

LOCATION

ICONS: 🚶 🐷 🪐 ✓   PRICE: $ $$ $$$ $$$$

THE FOOD

THE AMBIENCE

THE SERVICE

OTHER THOUGHTS

$ ($35 OR LESS FOR TWO) $$ ($35 TO $65 FOR TWO)
$$$ ($65 TO $100 FOR TWO) $$$$ (MORE THAN $100 FOR TWO)

☆ ☆ ☆ ☆

NAME   RATING

TYPE OF CUISINE

LOCATION

ICONS: 🧒 🐷 💘 ✓   PRICE: $ $$ $$$ $$$$

THE FOOD

THE AMBIENCE

THE SERVICE

OTHER THOUGHTS

$ ($35 OR LESS FOR TWO) $$ ($35 TO $65 FOR TWO)
$$$ ($65 TO $100 FOR TWO) $$$$ (MORE THAN $100 FOR TWO)

☆ ☆ ☆ ☆

NAME _____ RATING

TYPE OF CUISINE _____

LOCATION _____

ICONS: 🚶 🐷 💘 ✓   PRICE: $ $$ $$$ $$$$

THE FOOD
_____
_____
_____

THE AMBIENCE
_____
_____

THE SERVICE
_____

OTHER THOUGHTS
_____
_____
_____
_____
_____

$ ($35 OR LESS FOR TWO) $$ ($35 TO $65 FOR TWO)
$$$ ($65 TO $100 FOR TWO) $$$$ (MORE THAN $100 FOR TWO)

☆ ☆ ☆ ☆

NAME   RATING

TYPE OF CUISINE

LOCATION

ICONS: 👫 🐷 💘 ✓   PRICE: $ $$ $$$ $$$$

THE FOOD

THE AMBIENCE

THE SERVICE

OTHER THOUGHTS

$ ($35 OR LESS FOR TWO) $$ ($35 TO $65 FOR TWO)
$$$ ($65 TO $100 FOR TWO) $$$$ (MORE THAN $100 FOR TWO)

☆ ☆ ☆ ☆

NAME .... RATING

TYPE OF CUISINE ....

LOCATION ....

ICONS: 👫 🐷 💘 ✓   PRICE: $ $$ $$$ $$$$

THE FOOD
....

....

....

THE AMBIENCE
....

THE SERVICE
....

OTHER THOUGHTS
....

....

....

....

$ ($35 OR LESS FOR TWO) $$ ($35 TO $65 FOR TWO)
$$$ ($65 TO $100 FOR TWO) $$$$ (MORE THAN $100 FOR TWO)

☆ ☆ ☆ ☆
RATING

NAME
....

TYPE OF CUISINE
....

LOCATION
....

ICONS: 🚶 🍵 💘 ✓   PRICE: $ $$ $$$ $$$$

THE FOOD
....
....
....
....

THE AMBIENCE
....
....

THE SERVICE
....
....

OTHER THOUGHTS
....
....
....
....
....

$ ($35 OR LESS FOR TWO) $$ ($35 TO $65 FOR TWO)
$$$ ($65 TO $100 FOR TWO) $$$$ (MORE THAN $100 FOR TWO)

☆ ☆ ☆ ☆

NAME   RATING
....

TYPE OF CUISINE
....

LOCATION
....

ICONS: 👫 🫖 💘 ✔   PRICE: $ $$ $$$ $$$$

THE FOOD
....
....
....

THE AMBIENCE
....
....

THE SERVICE
....
....

OTHER THOUGHTS
....
....
....
....

$ ($35 OR LESS FOR TWO) $$ ($35 TO $65 FOR TWO)
$$$ ($65 TO $100 FOR TWO) $$$$ (MORE THAN $100 FOR TWO)

☆ ☆ ☆ ☆

NAME .... RATING

TYPE OF CUISINE ....

LOCATION ....

ICONS: 👫 🐷 💘 ✔   PRICE: $ $$ $$$ $$$$

THE FOOD

....

....

....

THE AMBIENCE

....

THE SERVICE

....

OTHER THOUGHTS

....

....

....

....

$ ($35 OR LESS FOR TWO) $$ ($35 TO $65 FOR TWO)
$$$ ($65 TO $100 FOR TWO) $$$$ (MORE THAN $100 FOR TWO)

☆ ☆ ☆ ☆

NAME   RATING

TYPE OF CUISINE

LOCATION

ICONS: 👫 🐷 💘 ✓   PRICE: $ $$ $$$ $$$$

THE FOOD

THE AMBIENCE

THE SERVICE

OTHER THOUGHTS

$ ($35 OR LESS FOR TWO) $$ ($35 TO $65 FOR TWO)
$$$ ($65 TO $100 FOR TWO) $$$$ (MORE THAN $100 FOR TWO)

☆ ☆ ☆ ☆

NAME   RATING

TYPE OF CUISINE

LOCATION

ICONS: 🏃 🐷 💘 ✓   PRICE: $ $$ $$$ $$$$

THE FOOD

THE AMBIENCE

THE SERVICE

OTHER THOUGHTS

$ ($35 OR LESS FOR TWO) $$ ($35 TO $65 FOR TWO)
$$$ ($65 TO $100 FOR TWO) $$$$ (MORE THAN $100 FOR TWO)

☆ ☆ ☆ ☆

NAME   RATING
....

TYPE OF CUISINE
....

LOCATION
....

ICONS: 👫 🐷 💘 ✔   PRICE: $ $$ $$$ $$$$

THE FOOD
....
....
....

THE AMBIENCE
....

THE SERVICE
....

OTHER THOUGHTS
....
....
....
....

$ ($35 OR LESS FOR TWO) $$ ($35 TO $65 FOR TWO)
$$$ ($65 TO $100 FOR TWO) $$$$ (MORE THAN $100 FOR TWO)

50

☆ ☆ ☆ ☆

NAME   RATING
....

TYPE OF CUISINE
....

LOCATION
....

ICONS: 👫 🐷 💘 ✓   PRICE: $ $$ $$$ $$$$

THE FOOD
....

....

....

THE AMBIENCE
....

....

THE SERVICE
....

....

OTHER THOUGHTS
....

....

....

....

....

$ ($35 OR LESS FOR TWO) $$ ($35 TO $65 FOR TWO)
$$$ ($65 TO $100 FOR TWO) $$$$ (MORE THAN $100 FOR TWO)

☆ ☆ ☆ ☆

NAME .... RATING

TYPE OF CUISINE ....

LOCATION ....

ICONS: 🧒 🫖 💘 ✓   PRICE: $ $$ $$$ $$$$

THE FOOD ....

....

....

....

THE AMBIENCE ....

....

THE SERVICE ....

....

OTHER THOUGHTS ....

....

....

....

....

$ ($35 OR LESS FOR TWO) $$ ($35 TO $65 FOR TWO)
$$$ ($65 TO $100 FOR TWO) $$$$ (MORE THAN $100 FOR TWO)

☆ ☆ ☆ ☆

NAME   RATING

TYPE OF CUISINE

LOCATION

ICONS: 🚻 🐷 💘 ✓   PRICE: $ $$ $$$ $$$$

THE FOOD

THE AMBIENCE

THE SERVICE

OTHER THOUGHTS

$ ($35 OR LESS FOR TWO) $$ ($35 TO $65 FOR TWO)
$$$ ($65 TO $100 FOR TWO) $$$$ (MORE THAN $100 FOR TWO)

☆ ☆ ☆ ☆

NAME   RATING

TYPE OF CUISINE

LOCATION

ICONS: 👫 🐷 💘 ✓   PRICE: $ $$ $$$ $$$$

THE FOOD

THE AMBIENCE

THE SERVICE

OTHER THOUGHTS

$ ($35 OR LESS FOR TWO) $$ ($35 TO $65 FOR TWO)
$$$ ($65 TO $100 FOR TWO) $$$$ (MORE THAN $100 FOR TWO)

$$\star\ \star\ \star\ \star$$

NAME

RATING

TYPE OF CUISINE

LOCATION

ICONS: 👫 🐷 💘 ✔   PRICE: $ $$ $$$ $$$$

THE FOOD

THE AMBIENCE

THE SERVICE

OTHER THOUGHTS

$ ($35 OR LESS FOR TWO) $$ ($35 TO $65 FOR TWO)
$$$ ($65 TO $100 FOR TWO) $$$$ (MORE THAN $100 FOR TWO)

☆ ☆ ☆ ☆

....

NAME   RATING

....

TYPE OF CUISINE

....

LOCATION

....

ICONS: 👫 🐷 🚀 ✓   PRICE: $ $$ $$$ $$$$

....

THE FOOD

....

....

....

THE AMBIENCE

....

THE SERVICE

....

OTHER THOUGHTS

....

....

....

....

$ ($35 OR LESS FOR TWO) $$ ($35 TO $65 FOR TWO)
$$$ ($65 TO $100 FOR TWO) $$$$ (MORE THAN $100 FOR TWO)

☆ ☆ ☆ ☆

NAME _____ RATING

TYPE OF CUISINE _____

LOCATION _____

ICONS: 👫 🐷 💘 ✓   PRICE: $ $$ $$$ $$$$

THE FOOD _____
_____
_____
_____

THE AMBIENCE _____
_____

THE SERVICE _____
_____

OTHER THOUGHTS _____
_____
_____
_____
_____

$ ($35 OR LESS FOR TWO) $$ ($35 TO $65 FOR TWO)
$$$ ($65 TO $100 FOR TWO) $$$$ (MORE THAN $100 FOR TWO)

57

☆ ☆ ☆ ☆

NAME   RATING

TYPE OF CUISINE

LOCATION

ICONS: 👫 🐷 💘 ✓   PRICE: $ $$ $$$ $$$$

THE FOOD

THE AMBIENCE

THE SERVICE

OTHER THOUGHTS

$ ($35 OR LESS FOR TWO) $$ ($35 TO $65 FOR TWO)
$$$ ($65 TO $100 FOR TWO) $$$$ (MORE THAN $100 FOR TWO)

☆ ☆ ☆ ☆

NAME .... RATING

TYPE OF CUISINE ....

LOCATION ....

ICONS: 🧑‍🧒   🐷   💘   ✓   PRICE: $ $$ $$$ $$$$

THE FOOD ....
....
....
....

THE AMBIENCE ....
....

THE SERVICE ....
....

OTHER THOUGHTS ....
....
....
....
....

$ ($35 OR LESS FOR TWO) $$ ($35 TO $65 FOR TWO)
$$$ ($65 TO $100 FOR TWO) $$$$ (MORE THAN $100 FOR TWO)

59

☆ ☆ ☆ ☆

NAME   RATING

TYPE OF CUISINE

LOCATION

ICONS: 👫 🫖 💘 ✓   PRICE: $ $$ $$$ $$$$

THE FOOD

THE AMBIENCE

THE SERVICE

OTHER THOUGHTS

$ ($35 OR LESS FOR TWO) $$ ($35 TO $65 FOR TWO)
$$$ ($65 TO $100 FOR TWO) $$$$ (MORE THAN $100 FOR TWO)

$\Large\star$ $\Large\star$ $\Large\star$ $\Large\star$

NAME .... RATING

TYPE OF CUISINE ....

LOCATION ....

ICONS: 👫 🐷 💘 ✓   PRICE: **$** **$$** **$$$** **$$$$**

THE FOOD
....
....
....

THE AMBIENCE
....

THE SERVICE
....

OTHER THOUGHTS
....
....
....
....
....

$ ($35 OR LESS FOR TWO) $$ ($35 TO $65 FOR TWO)
$$$ ($65 TO $100 FOR TWO) $$$$ (MORE THAN $100 FOR TWO)

☆ ☆ ☆ ☆

NAME

TYPE OF CUISINE

LOCATION

ICONS: 🚶‍♂️🚶 🫖 💘 ✓   PRICE: $ $$ $$$ $$$$

THE FOOD

THE AMBIENCE

THE SERVICE

OTHER THOUGHTS

$ ($35 OR LESS FOR TWO) $$ ($35 TO $65 FOR TWO)
$$$ ($65 TO $100 FOR TWO) $$$$ (MORE THAN $100 FOR TWO)

☆ ☆ ☆ ☆

NAME   RATING
....

TYPE OF CUISINE
....

LOCATION
....

ICONS: 🧒 🐷 💘 ✓   PRICE: $ $$ $$$ $$$$

THE FOOD
....
....
....

THE AMBIENCE
....

THE SERVICE
....

OTHER THOUGHTS
....
....
....
....

$ ($35 OR LESS FOR TWO) $$ ($35 TO $65 FOR TWO)
$$$ ($65 TO $100 FOR TWO) $$$$ (MORE THAN $100 FOR TWO)

☆ ☆ ☆ ☆

NAME   RATING

TYPE OF CUISINE

LOCATION

ICONS: 🧑‍🤝‍🧑   🐷   💘   ✓   PRICE: $ $$ $$$ $$$$

THE FOOD

THE AMBIENCE

THE SERVICE

OTHER THOUGHTS

$ ($35 OR LESS FOR TWO) $$ ($35 TO $65 FOR TWO)
$$$ ($65 TO $100 FOR TWO) $$$$ (MORE THAN $100 FOR TWO)

☆ ☆ ☆ ☆

NAME   RATING
....

TYPE OF CUISINE
....

LOCATION
....

ICONS: 🚻 🐷 💘 ✓   PRICE: $ $ $ $ $ $ $ $ $ $

THE FOOD
....
....
....

THE AMBIENCE
....

THE SERVICE
....

OTHER THOUGHTS
....
....
....
....
....

$ ($35 OR LESS FOR TWO) $$ ($35 TO $65 FOR TWO)
$$$ ($65 TO $100 FOR TWO) $$$$ (MORE THAN $100 FOR TWO)

☆ ☆ ☆ ☆

NAME RATING

TYPE OF CUISINE

LOCATION

ICONS: 👫 🐖 💘 ✓ PRICE: $ $$ $$$ $$$$

THE FOOD

THE AMBIENCE

THE SERVICE

OTHER THOUGHTS

$ ($35 OR LESS FOR TWO) $$ ($35 TO $65 FOR TWO)
$$$ ($65 TO $100 FOR TWO) $$$$ (MORE THAN $100 FOR TWO)

☆ ☆ ☆ ☆

NAME   RATING

TYPE OF CUISINE

LOCATION

ICONS: 👫 🐷 💘 ✓   PRICE: $ $$ $$$ $$$$

THE FOOD

THE AMBIENCE

THE SERVICE

OTHER THOUGHTS

$ ($35 OR LESS FOR TWO) $$ ($35 TO $65 FOR TWO)
$$$ ($65 TO $100 FOR TWO) $$$$ (MORE THAN $100 FOR TWO)

☆ ☆ ☆ ☆

NAME .... RATING

TYPE OF CUISINE ....

LOCATION ....

ICONS: 👫 🐷 🌶 ✔   PRICE: $ $$ $$$ $$$$

THE FOOD
....
....
....

THE AMBIENCE
....

THE SERVICE
....

OTHER THOUGHTS
....
....
....
....

$ ($35 OR LESS FOR TWO) $$ ($35 TO $65 FOR TWO)
$$$ ($65 TO $100 FOR TWO) $$$$ (MORE THAN $100 FOR TWO)

☆ ☆ ☆ ☆

NAME   RATING

TYPE OF CUISINE

LOCATION

ICONS: PRICE: $ $$ $$$ $$$$

THE FOOD

THE AMBIENCE

THE SERVICE

OTHER THOUGHTS

$ ($35 OR LESS FOR TWO) $$ ($35 TO $65 FOR TWO)
$$$ ($65 TO $100 FOR TWO) $$$$ (MORE THAN $100 FOR TWO)

☆ ☆ ☆ ☆

NAME   RATING

TYPE OF CUISINE

LOCATION

ICONS: 👫 🐷 💘 ✔   PRICE: $ $$ $$$ $$$$

THE FOOD

THE AMBIENCE

THE SERVICE

OTHER THOUGHTS

$ ($35 OR LESS FOR TWO) $$ ($35 TO $65 FOR TWO)
$$$ ($65 TO $100 FOR TWO) $$$$ (MORE THAN $100 FOR TWO)

☆ ☆ ☆ ☆

NAME   RATING
....

TYPE OF CUISINE
....

LOCATION
....

ICONS: 👫   🍲   💘   ✓   PRICE: $ $$ $$$ $$$$

....
THE FOOD
....

....

....

THE AMBIENCE
....

....

THE SERVICE
....

....

OTHER THOUGHTS
....

....

....

....

....

$ ($35 OR LESS FOR TWO) $$ ($35 TO $65 FOR TWO)
$$$ ($65 TO $100 FOR TWO) $$$$ (MORE THAN $100 FOR TWO)

☆ ☆ ☆ ☆

NAME   RATING

TYPE OF CUISINE

LOCATION

ICONS: 👫 🐷 💘 ✓   PRICE: $ $$ $$$ $$$$

THE FOOD

THE AMBIENCE

THE SERVICE

OTHER THOUGHTS

$ ($35 OR LESS FOR TWO) $$ ($35 TO $65 FOR TWO)
$$$ ($65 TO $100 FOR TWO) $$$$ (MORE THAN $100 FOR TWO)

☆ ☆ ☆ ☆

NAME   RATING

TYPE OF CUISINE

LOCATION

ICONS: 🚶 🐷 💘 ✓   PRICE: $ $$ $$$ $$$$

THE FOOD

THE AMBIENCE

THE SERVICE

OTHER THOUGHTS

$ ($35 OR LESS FOR TWO) $$ ($35 TO $65 FOR TWO)
$$$ ($65 TO $100 FOR TWO) $$$$ (MORE THAN $100 FOR TWO)

☆ ☆ ☆ ☆

NAME   RATING
....

TYPE OF CUISINE
....

LOCATION
....

ICONS: 🚶 🍲 💘 ✔   PRICE: $ $$ $$$ $$$$

THE FOOD
....
....
....

THE AMBIENCE
....

THE SERVICE
....

OTHER THOUGHTS
....
....
....
....

$ ($35 OR LESS FOR TWO) $$ ($35 TO $65 FOR TWO)
$$$ ($65 TO $100 FOR TWO) $$$$ (MORE THAN $100 FOR TWO)

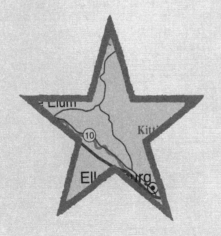

BEST PLACES TO STAY

☆ ☆ ☆ ☆

NAME   RATING

LOCATION

ICONS: 👫 🐷 💘 ✔   PRICE: $ $$ $$$ $$$$

THE ROOM

THE HOTEL

THE SERVICE

$ ($80 OR LESS PER NIGHT) $$ ($80 TO $120 PER NIGHT)
$$$ ($120 TO $200 PER NIGHT) $$$$ (MORE THAN $200 PER NIGHT)

THE TRIP

☆ ☆ ☆ ☆

NAME   RATING
....

LOCATION
....
....

ICONS: 🚻   🐷   💘   ✔   PRICE: $ $$ $$$ $$$$

THE ROOM
....
....
....
....
....

THE HOTEL
....
....
....

THE SERVICE
....
....

$ ($80 OR LESS PER NIGHT) $$ ($80 TO $120 PER NIGHT)
$$$ ($120 TO $200 PER NIGHT) $$$$ (MORE THAN $200 PER NIGHT)

THE TRIP

☆ ☆ ☆ ☆

NAME   RATING

LOCATION

ICONS: 👫 🐖 🚀 ✔   PRICE: $ $$ $$$ $$$$

THE ROOM

THE HOTEL

THE SERVICE

$ ($80 OR LESS PER NIGHT) $$ ($80 TO $120 PER NIGHT)
$$$ ($120 TO $200 PER NIGHT) $$$$ (MORE THAN $200 PER NIGHT)

THE TRIP

☆ ☆ ☆ ☆

NAME   RATING

LOCATION

ICONS: 👫 🐷 💘 ✓   PRICE: $ $$ $$$ $$$$

THE ROOM

THE HOTEL

THE SERVICE

$ ($80 OR LESS PER NIGHT) $$ ($80 TO $120 PER NIGHT)
$$$ ($120 TO $200 PER NIGHT) $$$$ (MORE THAN $200 PER NIGHT)

THE TRIP

☆ ☆ ☆ ☆

NAME   RATING

LOCATION

ICONS: 👫 🫖 💘 ✓   PRICE: $ $$ $$$ $$$$

THE ROOM

THE HOTEL

THE SERVICE

$ ($80 OR LESS PER NIGHT) $$ ($80 TO $120 PER NIGHT)
$$$ ($120 TO $200 PER NIGHT) $$$$ (MORE THAN $200 PER NIGHT)

THE TRIP

☆ ☆ ☆ ☆

NAME
                                                                    RATING

LOCATION

ICONS: 🧍🧍 🐖 ⚔   ✓   PRICE: $ $$ $$$ $$$$

THE ROOM

THE HOTEL

THE SERVICE

$ ($80 OR LESS PER NIGHT) $$ ($80 TO $120 PER NIGHT)
$$$ ($120 TO $200 PER NIGHT) $$$$ (MORE THAN $200 PER NIGHT)

THE TRIP

☆ ☆ ☆ ☆

NAME   RATING

LOCATION

ICONS: 🚶 🐷 💘 ✓   PRICE: $ $$ $$$ $$$$

THE ROOM

THE HOTEL

THE SERVICE

$ ($80 OR LESS PER NIGHT) $$ ($80 TO $120 PER NIGHT)
$$$ ($120 TO $200 PER NIGHT) $$$$ (MORE THAN $200 PER NIGHT)

THE TRIP

☆ ☆ ☆ ☆

NAME   RATING

LOCATION

....

ICONS: 👫 🫖 💘 ✔   PRICE: $ $$ $$$ $$$$

THE ROOM

....

....

....

....

THE HOTEL

....

....

THE SERVICE

....

....

$ ($80 OR LESS PER NIGHT) $$ ($80 TO $120 PER NIGHT)
$$$ ($120 TO $200 PER NIGHT) $$$$ (MORE THAN $200 PER NIGHT)

THE TRIP

☆ ☆ ☆ ☆
RATING

NAME

LOCATION

ICONS: 👫 🐷 🪐 ✔   PRICE: $ $$ $$$ $$$$

THE ROOM

THE HOTEL

THE SERVICE

$ ($80 OR LESS PER NIGHT) $$ ($80 TO $120 PER NIGHT)
$$$ ($120 TO $200 PER NIGHT) $$$$ (MORE THAN $200 PER NIGHT)

THE TRIP

☆ ☆ ☆ ☆

NAME   RATING

LOCATION

ICONS: 🚶 🐷 💘 ✓   PRICE: $ $$ $$$ $$$$

THE ROOM

THE HOTEL

THE SERVICE

$ ($80 OR LESS PER NIGHT) $$ ($80 TO $120 PER NIGHT)
$$$ ($120 TO $200 PER NIGHT) $$$$ (MORE THAN $200 PER NIGHT)

THE TRIP

☆ ☆ ☆ ☆

NAME   RATING

LOCATION

ICONS: 👫   🐷   💘   ✔   PRICE: $ $$ $$$ $$$$

THE ROOM

THE HOTEL

THE SERVICE

$ ($80 OR LESS PER NIGHT) $$ ($80 TO $120 PER NIGHT)
$$$ ($120 TO $200 PER NIGHT) $$$$ (MORE THAN $200 PER NIGHT)

THE TRIP

☆ ☆ ☆ ☆

NAME .... RATING

LOCATION ....

....

ICONS: 👫 🏺 💘 ✓   PRICE: $ $$ $$$ $$$$

THE ROOM ....

....

....

....

....

....

THE HOTEL ....

....

....

....

THE SERVICE ....

....

....

$ ($80 OR LESS PER NIGHT) $$ ($80 TO $120 PER NIGHT)
$$$ ($120 TO $200 PER NIGHT) $$$$ (MORE THAN $200 PER NIGHT)

THE TRIP

☆ ☆ ☆ ☆

NAME   RATING

LOCATION

ICONS: 👫 🐷 💘 ✔   PRICE: $ $$ $$$ $$$$

THE ROOM

THE HOTEL

THE SERVICE

$ ($80 OR LESS PER NIGHT) $$ ($80 TO $120 PER NIGHT)
$$$ ($120 TO $200 PER NIGHT) $$$$ (MORE THAN $200 PER NIGHT)

THE TRIP

☆ ☆ ☆ ☆

NAME   RATING

LOCATION

ICONS: 👫 🐖 💘 ✓   PRICE: $ $$ $$$ $$$$

THE ROOM

THE HOTEL

THE SERVICE

$ ($80 OR LESS PER NIGHT) $$ ($80 TO $120 PER NIGHT)
$$$ ($120 TO $200 PER NIGHT) $$$$ (MORE THAN $200 PER NIGHT)

THE TRIP

☆ ☆ ☆ ☆

NAME   RATING

LOCATION

ICONS: 👫 🐷 💘 ✓   PRICE: $ $$ $$$ $$$$

THE ROOM

THE HOTEL

THE SERVICE

$ ($80 OR LESS PER NIGHT) $$ ($80 TO $120 PER NIGHT)
$$$ ($120 TO $200 PER NIGHT) $$$$ (MORE THAN $200 PER NIGHT)

THE TRIP

☆ ☆ ☆ ☆

NAME
RATING
....

LOCATION
....

....

....

ICONS: PRICE: $ $$ $$$ $$$$

THE ROOM
....

....

....

....

....

....

THE HOTEL
....

....

....

THE SERVICE
....

....

....

$ ($80 OR LESS PER NIGHT) $$ ($80 TO $120 PER NIGHT)
$$$ ($120 TO $200 PER NIGHT) $$$$ (MORE THAN $200 PER NIGHT)

THE TRIP

☆ ☆ ☆ ☆

NAME   RATING

LOCATION

ICONS: 🚹 🐷 🚀 ✔   PRICE: $ $$ $$$ $$$$

THE ROOM

THE HOTEL

THE SERVICE

$ ($80 OR LESS PER NIGHT) $$ ($80 TO $120 PER NIGHT)
$$$ ($120 TO $200 PER NIGHT) $$$$ (MORE THAN $200 PER NIGHT)

THE TRIP

☆ ☆ ☆ ☆

NAME   RATING

LOCATION

ICONS: 🧒🧒 🐷 💘 ✓   PRICE: $ $$ $$$ $$$$

THE ROOM

THE HOTEL

THE SERVICE

$ ($80 OR LESS PER NIGHT) $$ ($80 TO $120 PER NIGHT)
$$$ ($120 TO $200 PER NIGHT) $$$$ (MORE THAN $200 PER NIGHT)

THE TRIP

☆ ☆ ☆ ☆

NAME   RATING
....

LOCATION
....

....

ICONS: 👫 🐷 🪐 ✓   PRICE: $ $$ $$$ $$$$

THE ROOM
....

....

....

....

....

THE HOTEL
....

....

THE SERVICE
....

....

$ ($80 OR LESS PER NIGHT) $$ ($80 TO $120 PER NIGHT)
$$$ ($120 TO $200 PER NIGHT) $$$$ (MORE THAN $200 PER NIGHT)

THE TRIP

BEST PLACES TO SHOP

☆ ☆ ☆ ☆

NAME .... RATING

TYPE OF STORE ....

LOCATION ....

WHY GO ....

MY WISH LIST ....

....

....

★ ★

☆ ☆ ☆ ☆

NAME .... RATING

TYPE OF STORE ....

LOCATION ....

WHY GO ....

MY WISH LIST ....

....

....

116

☆ ☆ ☆ ☆

NAME .... RATING

TYPE OF STORE ....

LOCATION ....

....

WHY GO ....

....

MY WISH LIST ....

....

....

....

* *

☆ ☆ ☆ ☆

NAME .... RATING

TYPE OF STORE ....

LOCATION ....

....

WHY GO ....

....

MY WISH LIST ....

....

....

☆ ☆ ☆ ☆

RATING

NAME

TYPE OF STORE

LOCATION

WHY GO

MY WISH LIST

* *

☆ ☆ ☆ ☆

RATING

NAME

TYPE OF STORE

LOCATION

WHY GO

MY WISH LIST

☆ ☆ ☆ ☆

NAME .... RATING

TYPE OF STORE ....

LOCATION ....

....

WHY GO ....

....

MY WISH LIST ....

....

....

....

* *

☆ ☆ ☆ ☆

NAME .... RATING

TYPE OF STORE ....

LOCATION ....

....

WHY GO ....

....

MY WISH LIST ....

....

....

....

☆ ☆ ☆ ☆

RATING

NAME

....

TYPE OF STORE

....

LOCATION

....

....

WHY GO

....

....

MY WISH LIST

....

....

....

....

★ ★

☆ ☆ ☆ ☆

RATING

NAME

....

TYPE OF STORE

....

LOCATION

....

....

WHY GO

....

....

MY WISH LIST

....

....

....

☆ ☆ ☆ ☆

NAME .... RATING

TYPE OF STORE ....

LOCATION ....

....

WHY GO ....

....

MY WISH LIST ....

....

....

....

* *

☆ ☆ ☆ ☆

NAME .... RATING

TYPE OF STORE ....

LOCATION ....

....

WHY GO ....

....

MY WISH LIST ....

....

....

☆ ☆ ☆ ☆

NAME .... RATING

TYPE OF STORE ....

LOCATION ....

WHY GO ....

MY WISH LIST ....

....

....

★ ★

☆ ☆ ☆ ☆

NAME .... RATING

TYPE OF STORE ....

LOCATION ....

WHY GO ....

MY WISH LIST ....

....

....

☆ ☆ ☆ ☆

NAME

RATING

TYPE OF STORE

LOCATION

WHY GO

MY WISH LIST

* *

☆ ☆ ☆ ☆

NAME

RATING

TYPE OF STORE

LOCATION

WHY GO

MY WISH LIST

☆ ☆ ☆ ☆

NAME .... RATING

TYPE OF STORE ....

LOCATION ....
....

WHY GO ....
....

MY WISH LIST ....
....
....
....

* *

☆ ☆ ☆ ☆

NAME .... RATING

TYPE OF STORE ....

LOCATION ....
....

WHY GO ....
....

MY WISH LIST ....
....
....

☆ ☆ ☆ ☆

NAME .... RATING

TYPE OF STORE ....

LOCATION ....

....

WHY GO ....

....

MY WISH LIST ....

....

....

....

★ ★

☆ ☆ ☆ ☆

NAME .... RATING

TYPE OF STORE ....

LOCATION ....

....

WHY GO ....

....

MY WISH LIST ....

....

....

☆ ☆ ☆ ☆

NAME .... RATING

TYPE OF STORE ....

LOCATION ....

....

WHY GO ....

....

MY WISH LIST ....

....

....

....

★ ★

☆ ☆ ☆ ☆

NAME .... RATING

TYPE OF STORE ....

LOCATION ....

....

WHY GO ....

....

MY WISH LIST ....

....

....

☆ ☆ ☆ ☆
NAME .... RATING

TYPE OF STORE ....

LOCATION ....

....

WHY GO ....

....

MY WISH LIST ....

....

....

....

★ ★

☆ ☆ ☆ ☆
NAME .... RATING

TYPE OF STORE ....

LOCATION ....

....

WHY GO ....

....

MY WISH LIST ....

....

....

....

☆ ☆ ☆ ☆

NAME .... RATING

TYPE OF STORE ....

LOCATION ....

WHY GO ....

MY WISH LIST ....

★ ★

☆ ☆ ☆ ☆

NAME .... RATING

TYPE OF STORE ....

LOCATION ....

WHY GO ....

MY WISH LIST ....

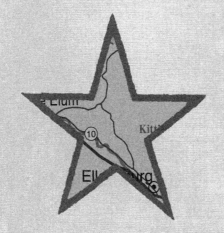

MORE BEST PLACES

RESOURCES

WEB SITES

www.alaskaair.com/destinations
City guides and resources for travelers.

www.brownpapertickets.com
The first and only fair-trade ticketing service.

www.cheaptickets.com
Cheap flights, hotels, vacations, last-minute trips, rental cars, and cruises.

cityguide.aol.com
Restaurants, events, entertainment, concerts, tickets, movies, hotels, and weather.

www.citysearch.com
Recommendations and reviews for restaurants, bars & clubs, hotels, shopping, beauty, movies, events, and more.

www.dexonline.com
Yellow pages and online phone book.

www.kayak.com
Airfares, hotel reservations, and car rentals.

local.yahoo.com
Find business and services near you.

www.nearlocal.com
Local directory, city guide, and reviews.

www.olcg.com
Online City Guide—maps, hotels, car rentals, airlines, cruises, and tickets.

www.openlist.com
Restaurant and hotel guide.

www.travelocity.com
Airfares, hotels, vacations, cruises, car rentals, and more.

www.urban-pages.com
A guide for city dwellers looking for local information.

www.yelp.com
Reviews for restaurants, shopping, nightlife, spas, salons, and more.

FOOD/WINE/BEER PAIRINGS

TYPE OF FOOD	WINE PAIRING	BEER PAIRING
Beef, veal	Cabernet Sauvignon, Merlot, Bordeaux, Syrah	Porter, Pale or Amber Ale, Stout
Chicken	Chardonnay, Pinot Blanc, Pinot Noir	Lager, Pilsner, Porter
Pork	Pinot Noir, Riesling, Chardonnay	Lager, Fruity Ale, Porter
Lamb	Bordeaux, Cabernet Sauvignon, Merlot	Pale Ale, Porter, Stout
Game birds	Pinot Noir, Cabernet Sauvignon, Riesling, Zinfandel	Fruity Pale Ale, Brown Ale
Seafood, fish	Chardonnay, Sauvignon Blanc, Pinot Noir, Syrah	Stout, India Pale Ale, Hefeweizen, Pilsner
Pasta with tomato sauce	Chianti, Cabernet Sauvignon, White Zinfandel	Amber, Lager, Dunkel Lager
Pasta with butter/cream sauce	Chardonnay, Sauvignon Blanc	Pilsner, Cream Stout
Vegetarian dishes	Pinot Noir, Sauvignon Blanc, Champagne	Pilsner, Lager, Pale Ale
Salads, soups	Rosé, Champagne, Riesling, Sauvignon Blanc	Dunkel Lager, Hefeweizen, Brown Ale, Pilsner
Cheeses	Pinot Noir, Merlot, Sherry	Old Ale, Porter, Stout, Hefeweizen
Spicy foods	Riesling, Champagne	Lager, Pilsner, India Pale Ale
Barbeque	Syrah, Zinfandel	Pale or Amber Ale, Lager
Desserts	Port, Framboise, Merlot	Cream Stout, Doppelbock, Fruity Ale

TIP GUIDE

BILL TOTAL	15% TIP	20% TIP
$ 5.00	$ 0.75	$ 1.00
10.00	1.50	2.00
15.00	2.25	3.00
20.00	3.00	4.00
25.00	3.75	5.00
30.00	4.50	6.00
35.00	5.25	7.00
40.00	6.00	8.00
45.00	6.75	9.00
50.00	7.50	10.00
55.00	8.25	11.00
60.00	9.00	12.00
65.00	9.75	13.00
70.00	10.50	14.00
75.00	11.25	15.00
80.00	12.00	16.00
85.00	12.75	17.00
90.00	13.50	18.00
95.00	14.25	19.00
100.00	15.00	20.00
105.00	15.75	21.00
110.00	16.50	22.00
115.00	17.25	23.00
120.00	18.00	24.00
125.00	18.75	25.00
150.00	22.50	30.00
175.00	26.25	35.00
200.00	30.00	40.00
225.00	33.75	45.00
250.00	37.50	50.00
275.00	41.25	55.00
300.00	45.00	60.00

THREE-YEAR CALENDAR
2008

JANUARY

S	M	Tu	W	Th	F	S
		1	2	3	4	5
6	7	8	9	10	11	12
13	14	15	16	17	18	19
20	21	22	23	24	25	26
27	28	29	30	31		

FEBRUARY

S	M	Tu	W	Th	F	S
					1	2
3	4	5	6	7	8	9
10	11	12	13	14	15	16
17	18	19	20	21	22	23
24	25	26	27	28	29	

MARCH

S	M	Tu	W	Th	F	S
						1
2	3	4	5	6	7	8
9	10	11	12	13	14	15
16	17	18	19	20	21	22
23	24	25	26	27	28	29
30	31					

APRIL

S	M	Tu	W	Th	F	S
		1	2	3	4	5
6	7	8	9	10	11	12
13	14	15	16	17	18	19
20	21	22	23	24	25	26
27	28	29	30			

MAY

S	M	Tu	W	Th	F	S
				1	2	3
4	5	6	7	8	9	10
11	12	13	14	15	16	17
18	19	20	21	22	23	24
25	26	27	28	29	30	31

JUNE

S	M	Tu	W	Th	F	S
1	2	3	4	5	6	7
8	9	10	11	12	13	14
15	16	17	18	19	20	21
22	23	24	25	26	27	28
29	30					

JULY

S	M	Tu	W	Th	F	S
		1	2	3	4	5
6	7	8	9	10	11	12
13	14	15	16	17	18	19
20	21	22	23	24	25	26
27	28	29	30	31		

AUGUST

S	M	Tu	W	Th	F	S
					1	2
3	4	5	6	7	8	9
10	11	12	13	14	15	16
17	18	19	20	21	22	23
24	25	26	27	28	29	30
31						

SEPTEMBER

S	M	Tu	W	Th	F	S
	1	2	3	4	5	6
7	8	9	10	11	12	13
14	15	16	17	18	19	20
21	22	23	24	25	26	27
28	29	30				

OCTOBER

S	M	Tu	W	Th	F	S
			1	2	3	4
5	6	7	8	9	10	11
12	13	14	15	16	17	18
19	20	21	22	23	24	25
26	27	28	29	30	31	

NOVEMBER

S	M	Tu	W	Th	F	S
						1
2	3	4	5	6	7	8
9	10	11	12	13	14	15
16	17	18	19	20	21	22
23	24	25	26	27	28	29
30						

DECEMBER

S	M	Tu	W	Th	F	S
	1	2	3	4	5	6
7	8	9	10	11	12	13
14	15	16	17	18	19	20
21	22	23	24	25	26	27
28	29	30	31			

2009

JANUARY

S	M	Tu	W	Th	F	S
				1	2	3
4	5	6	7	8	9	10
11	12	13	14	15	16	17
18	19	20	21	22	23	24
25	26	27	28	29	30	31

FEBRUARY

S	M	Tu	W	Th	F	S
1	2	3	4	5	6	7
8	9	10	11	12	13	14
15	16	17	18	19	20	21
22	23	24	25	26	27	28

MARCH

S	M	Tu	W	Th	F	S
1	2	3	4	5	6	7
8	9	10	11	12	13	14
15	16	17	18	19	20	21
22	23	24	25	26	27	28
29	30	31				

APRIL

S	M	Tu	W	Th	F	S
			1	2	3	4
5	6	7	8	9	10	11
12	13	14	15	16	17	18
19	20	21	22	23	24	25
26	27	28	29	30		

MAY

S	M	Tu	W	Th	F	S
					1	2
3	4	5	6	7	8	9
10	11	12	13	14	15	16
17	18	19	20	21	22	23
24	25	26	27	28	29	30
31						

JUNE

S	M	Tu	W	Th	F	S
	1	2	3	4	5	6
7	8	9	10	11	12	13
14	15	16	17	18	19	20
21	22	23	24	25	26	27
28	29	30				

JULY

S	M	Tu	W	Th	F	S
			1	2	3	4
5	6	7	8	9	10	11
12	13	14	15	16	17	18
19	20	21	22	23	24	25
26	27	28	29	30	31	

AUGUST

S	M	Tu	W	Th	F	S
						1
2	3	4	5	6	7	8
9	10	11	12	13	14	15
16	17	18	19	20	21	22
23	24	25	26	27	28	29
30	31					

SEPTEMBER

S	M	Tu	W	Th	F	S
		1	2	3	4	5
6	7	8	9	10	11	12
13	14	15	16	17	18	19
20	21	22	23	24	25	26
27	28	29	30			

OCTOBER

S	M	Tu	W	Th	F	S
				1	2	3
4	5	6	7	8	9	10
11	12	13	14	15	16	17
18	19	20	21	22	23	24
25	26	27	28	29	30	31

NOVEMBER

S	M	Tu	W	Th	F	S
1	2	3	4	5	6	7
8	9	10	11	12	13	14
15	16	17	18	19	20	21
22	23	24	25	26	27	28
29	30					

DECEMBER

S	M	Tu	W	Th	F	S
		1	2	3	4	5
6	7	8	9	10	11	12
13	14	15	16	17	18	19
20	21	22	23	24	25	26
27	28	29	30	31		

2010

JANUARY

S	M	Tu	W	Th	F	S
					1	2
3	4	5	6	7	8	9
10	11	12	13	14	15	16
17	18	19	20	21	22	23
24	25	26	27	28	29	30
31						

FEBRUARY

S	M	Tu	W	Th	F	S
	1	2	3	4	5	6
7	8	9	10	11	12	13
14	15	16	17	18	19	20
21	22	23	24	25	26	27
28						

MARCH

S	M	Tu	W	Th	F	S
	1	2	3	4	5	6
7	8	9	10	11	12	13
14	15	16	17	18	19	20
21	22	23	24	25	26	27
28	29	30	31			

APRIL

S	M	Tu	W	Th	F	S
				1	2	3
4	5	6	7	8	9	10
11	12	13	14	15	16	17
18	19	20	21	22	23	24
25	26	27	28	29	30	

MAY

S	M	Tu	W	Th	F	S
						1
2	3	4	5	6	7	8
9	10	11	12	13	14	15
16	17	18	19	20	21	22
23	24	25	26	27	28	29
30	31					

JUNE

S	M	Tu	W	Th	F	S
		1	2	3	4	5
6	7	8	9	10	11	12
13	14	15	16	17	18	19
20	21	22	23	24	25	26
27	28	29	30			

JULY

S	M	Tu	W	Th	F	S
				1	2	3
4	5	6	7	8	9	10
11	12	13	14	15	16	17
18	19	20	21	22	23	24
25	26	27	28	29	30	31

AUGUST

S	M	Tu	W	Th	F	S
1	2	3	4	5	6	7
8	9	10	11	12	13	14
15	16	17	18	19	20	21
22	23	24	25	26	27	28
29	30	31				

SEPTEMBER

S	M	Tu	W	Th	F	S
			1	2	3	4
5	6	7	8	9	10	11
12	13	14	15	16	17	18
19	20	21	22	23	24	25
26	27	28	29	30		

OCTOBER

S	M	Tu	W	Th	F	S
					1	2
3	4	5	6	7	8	9
10	11	12	13	14	15	16
17	18	19	20	21	22	23
24	25	26	27	28	29	30
31						

NOVEMBER

S	M	Tu	W	Th	F	S
	1	2	3	4	5	6
7	8	9	10	11	12	13
14	15	16	17	18	19	20
21	22	23	24	25	26	27
28	29	30				

DECEMBER

S	M	Tu	W	Th	F	S
			1	2	3	4
5	6	7	8	9	10	11
12	13	14	15	16	17	18
19	20	21	22	23	24	25
26	27	28	29	30	31	

Find Your **Best Places**®

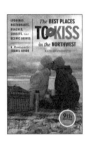

TITLE	AUTHOR	PRICE
Best Places Alaska, 3rd ed.	Ripley	21.95
Best Places Northwest, 16th ed.	Farhat	21.00
Best Places Portland, 6th ed.	Gottberg	19.95
Best Places Seattle, 10th ed.	O'Leary	18.95
Best Places Vancouver, 4th ed.	Wilson	18.95
Best Places to Kiss in the Northwest, 9th ed.	Chynoweth	21.00
Best Places to Kiss in Northern California, 6th ed.	Chynoweth	21.00
Best Places to Kiss in Southern California, 5th ed.	Steele	21.00

ALL **BEST PLACES**® GUIDEBOOKS ARE AVAILABLE AT BOOKSTORES EVERYWHERE.

SASQUATCH BOOKS
www.sasquatchbooks.com

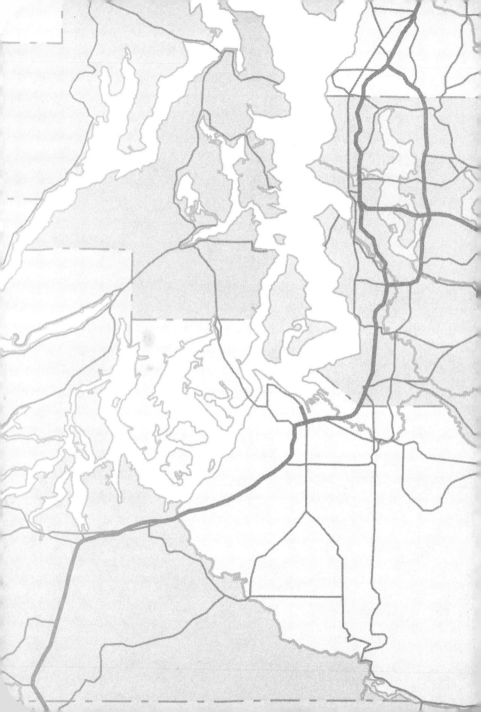